Also by Jason Baldinger:

The Whiskey Rebellion w/ Jerome Crooks (Six Gallery Press)
The Lady Pittsburgh (Speed and Briscoe Press)
The Lower Forty-Eight (Six Gallery Press)
The Studs Terkel Blues (Nightballet Press)
Fumbles Revelations (Grackle and Crow)
This Useless Beauty (Alien Buddha Press)
The Ugly Side of the Lake w/ John Dorsey (Nightballet Press)
The Better Angels of our Nature (Kung Fu Treachery Press)
Blind into Leaving (Analog Submission Press)
A Threadbare Universe (Kung Fu Treachery Press)
The Afterlife is a Hangover (Stubborn Mule Press)
The Nu Profit$ of P/O/E/T/I/C Di$chord: *And Even if we
Did, So What!?* (OAC Book w/ Damian Rucci,
Shawn Pavey, Nathaniel Stolte
A History of Backroads Misplaced: Selected Poems 2010-2020
(Kung Fu Treachery)
Little Fires Hiding w/ James Benger (Kung Fu Treachery Press)
Everyone's Alone Tonight w/ James Benger (Kung Fu Treachery Press)
This Still Life w/ James Benger (Kung Fu Treachery Press)
Topography of Disappearing (Between Shadows Press)
Don't Spook the Armadillo (La Belle Riviere Press)
Lazarus (Photographs) (OAC Press)

Waiting on Hummingbirds

Poems by Jason Baldinger
and James Benger

Kung Fu Treachery Press

Rancho Cucamonga, California

Copyright © Jason Baldinger, James Benger, 2024

First Edition: 1 3 5 7 9 10 8 6 4 2

ISBN: 978-1-958182-82-6

LCCN: 2024944452

Cover image: Jon Dowling

Title page image: Jason Baldinger

Author photos: Ed Teach

Acknowledgments

Special thanks go to the editors of the following publications where these poems first appeared:

Alien Buddha Zine: "the excommunication of bob," *Angels on a Sylvan Road:* "incremental," *The Angel's Share:* "Edge," "He Calls It a Life," *As It Ought to Be:* "cold water glistens," "the aforementioned skyline," "the last vestige of tiki," *Blast Furnace:* "The Old Girl," *I-70 Review:* "chuck taylors," "Corners," "Bright as the Darkness," "Drive," "Driveway Gravel," *North of Oxford:* "the bay city blues," "to live as the moon," *Ovation:* "the half life of lead," *Red Fez:* "god is back in town," *Rye Whiskey Review:* "hymn to a pittsburgh toilet," *Trailer Park Quarterly:* "11:59," "Grayson, MO," "Halloween 1988," "tear," "vocal," *Vox Populi:* "a howard johnson prayer," *The Writers Place Yearbook:* "Legacy"

James thanks Jason for always being willing to do this again, and for always presenting me with work that forces me to push myself, Jason Ryberg for continuing to give our books a home, the editors of *Blast Furnace, I-70 Review, The Angel's Share, Trailer Park Quarterly,* and *The Writers Place Yearbook* for giving many of my poems in this collection their first home, the poets of 365 Poems in 365 Days who are constantly pummeled with my first drafts, and Dad, Hannah, Milo, and Felix.

Jason thanks James for keeping these long distance letters flowing, I look forward to doing these books! I'd also like to thank Jason Ryberg, John Dorsey, Victor Clevenger, Osage Arts Community, Bob Pajich, Jon Dowling, Scott Silsbe and apologies for those I may have forgotten to mention.

Table of Contents:

Part I: The Moment's Overrated

Drive / 1

train whistle morning / 2

chuck taylors / 3

to live as the moon / 4

Halloween 1988 / 5

the excommunication of bob / 8

Bright as the Darkness / 11

the current of grasshoppers / 12

Driveway Gravel / 13

cold water glistens / 15

Legacy / 16

when noise was young / 18

Interlude: Dreaming

The Old Girl / 23

the bay city blues / 25

Part II: Searching for a Reason

Getting On / 29

phil ochs' suicide note / 31

He Calls It a Life / 33

barely living patriots / 36

Edge / 38

the last vestige of tiki / 40

11:59 / 42

god is back in town / 44

Dust / 46

half life of lead / 47

Corners / 49

a narrative of bloodshot / 50

tear / 52

hymn to a pittsburgh toilet / 54

vocal / 56

black and white dreams / 58

Part III: What We Have

incremental / 63

a howard johnson prayer / 65

disposable / 66

the aforementioned skyline / 67

Grayson, MO / 69

sixty-cycle hum / 70

Spiral / 72

across grayscale scrub / 74

Inventory / 76

a time capsule of dust / 77

lonesome sinner, lonesome saint,
make me winner, before it's too late

       -ass ponys, *dollar a day*

You've broken the speed of the sound of loneliness
You're out there running just to be on the run

       -John Prine, *Speed of the Sound*
         of Lonliness

Part I
The Moment's Overrated

Drive

Let me follow you to everywhere.
I've had practice in being an
easy traveling companion.
I'll go wherever, so long as you're there,
maybe let me take the wheel now and then.
The rubber's good,
and I'll guide you through the
breathing white clouds of gravel roads.
I love those star-filled, electricless nights,
but on occasion, I can see the excitement
in your neon existence too.
It all has a place;
counterbalance.
We don't need anything but ourselves
and the road.
I can change a tire, and the oil,
and smell a dying solenoid
at least a couple miles away.
Pens are for writing home;
telling lies and the truth in one breath.
I saw you in a dream so many years ago,
so get in the driver's seat,
I'll be your passenger,
let's go open it all.

-Benger

train whistle morning

counting down
another county line
waiting on the buffalo
these signs promised

the slow education of power lines
I don't know how many rivers crossed
insert an inventory of place
now count the waters with me

I almost graze a hawk
rabbit in peril's talons
november evening swells
the earth strives for dormant

weather at my heels
gasoline drips down chin
a barred owl perched
on a gut shot speed marker
an el camino in a dollar store lot

red echo of brake lights
second roses of a motel season
fog lays across railroad tracks
a time zone in either direction
frostbit in a train whistle morning

-baldinger

chuck taylors

we had endless summer moments
embraced in the pheromonal thrill of it all
nights when blue gave way only to green
and everything rolled sweet in the hills

rusted billboard poles and
busted no trespassing placards meant nothing
to midnight abandon

and our thin wallets grew thinner
on the lust of adventure

there is a smell of the air
around a gas pump at two a m
when you're sixteen and have
nowhere
no one
to be
it smells like the memories that will be buried
until one chance day they're not
and the blood will boil again
in the sweet simmer of freedom

keys turned easy in ignitions
and secrets were locked away in the trunk
the backseat cried for more
and the sunrise on the horizon

always looked its most beautiful
through a cracked windshield

-Benger

to live as the moon

those shifts were interminable
pallet jack drags tons
across industrial tile floors
a wasteland of consumable goods
halogen glare in the hell of four am

from november til april
there was no such thing as daylight
driving east into sunrise before
a couple miller genuines
an episode of CHiPS
to live as the moon
seasonal depression as a shadow

summers were death
playgrounds outside buzz
lawnmowers of regular hours
full hot breath of humidity
resting on your chest
as deep sleep should settle
wake in sweat, with afternoon bright
the only pleasure found in ice cold water
head in full swell of open tap
brief indulgence before stillness
evaporate back to sleep
always another shift
waiting

-baldinger

Halloween 1988

Dad dressed me up in his clothes,
complete with gun belt and hat
(wouldn't give me a real pistol, though)
said:
"There, you're a cowboy,"
and off we went,
our first time for real trick or treating
(Halloweenin as Dad called it).

It all felt so official,
the first time living in a real neighborhood,
with actual neighbors,
and a city-ordained septic tank,
and mailboxes and stuff.
It felt like we'd finally made it,
and we were going to
live like those folks on the tv.

We ambled down the gravel road,
parents trailing a little behind,
knocking doors, marveling at
Halloween candy that wasn't the
mints from the dish at the Pizza Hut
in town where Mom waitressed.
We went all the way to where
gravel Marquette Avenue butted up with
paved Clinton Street, then turned around.

Our last stop was the trailer
across the gravel from our place.
We'd only been in the neighborhood
a couple months, but the
blue and white singlewide
had been there even less.
The owners invited us in.
He was a shirtless skinny man
with an impressive brown mullet,
and she was the epitome of
late eighties hairspray queen.
I remember a year or so after that night,
she came over to our place
when I had the flu to make sure
I was drinking enough orange juice.

The trailer was sparsely furnished;
two chairs and a coffee table.
A half dozen varieties of
dollar store candy
amidst a hastily swept dusting of something
I no longer think was confectioner's sugar.
There was a giant deer head
mounted to the dimly lit
faux wood panel wall.

I asked the man where the buck came from.
He said:
"Done got me that one.
Put up one bitch of a fight, though"
I asked where the rest of the animal was.
"Oh, he's out there. Whyn'tcha go on out,
make sure his backside's still there."

I did and it wasn't.

Not long after that,
Mom and Dad got us out of there fast.
My brother walked off with
an entire bag of circus peanuts.
I forgot my candy.

                    -Benger

the excommunication of bob

shake it off in front
of the porcelain face
of the downstairs
men's room urinal
when they burst in

bob zientara pushed
by a troop of teenage boys
they jam into the stall
crowd for vantage

I squeeze through bottleneck
try to understand
this masculine hoopla

for weeks study hall
became the olympics of top that
tearing phone books in half
grab ass and charley horses

then shit got dark
bloody knuckles
with sharpened
fifty cent pieces
the boys started
trading blood and pain
for money

bob agreed to a new dare
he'd bite the head off
a live white mouse
boys froth
he takes his place
above the bowl

mouse appears
to a blood sermon
to rising cheers

I am not a gladiator
rush out as a moment shatters
as testosterone crescendos

mouse and head separated
swirl unceremoniously to sewers
boys later boasted of
blood streaked on bob's teeth

I still root for the mouse
replay the moment
except as the mouse realizes its fate
it yawns
blinks twice
before opening its jaws
human sized
swallowing bob
before a crowd of silent
stunned teenage centurions

catholic school is a strange place
martyred education
around core values
of guilt and shame

the principal
attracted by the noise of a blood sacrifice
of a twisted ritual of manhood
she was in the hall
as the bathroom cleared
bob and others were caught
some were expelled
bob, he was excommunicated

-baldinger

Bright as the Darkness

On moonshot nights
we ran, flashlights and
shorts, brambles and
boots.

The goal was to go as
deep, as unseen, as
completely immersed in
forest green isolation,
to hear the cicadas and
the coyotes duet while
autumn leaves were
coaxed by the wind to
provide the cool jazz
backbeat.

Lights out with early
dew drops and morning
glory spiders crawling,
crawling to find a home,
closed eyes and communion,
total envelopment, breathing
the universe.

Unused tents pitched over
blue plastic tarps, a ring of
stones for a fire that would
never glow half as bright
as the darkness of the moon
on a starless night.

-Benger

the current of grasshoppers

this goldenrod ocean
tide in, wade to belly
tide out, brushed with pollen

a wake of three hawks
a horizon rimmed in clouds
a honeybee dunked drunk
a dragonfly's fleeting concern
a fragment web breezes

I lay down another collection of miles
on a sun warmed rock
for spiders to make
of as they choose

here to settle a moment
after another whirlwind
after this head turned inside out
metallic silver dreams leaked free

a moment reforming
all matter and matters negotiable
a still life in the current of grasshoppers

-baldinger

Driveway Gravel

We would ride like hell
in Mom's '77 Diplomat,
me behind the wheel,
we pretended we were
the Duke boys as we
jumped imaginary gullies,
hood ornament glinting in the
white July sun.

Mom'd yell at us
from the kitchen window
as we wriggled out the windows
instead of using doors;
the glass didn't roll down all the way,
she was sure we'd end up
cut and sorry.

Sometimes when she was away
at whatever factory
the temp agency sent her to,
and Dad was inside
doing his best to
sleep off a twelve hour night shift,
I'd throw the wagon in neutral,
let her inch back to the dusty line
where the gravel driveway
met the hardpacked dirt of
Marquette Avenue.

Windows down,
the crunch of those white rocks
under the bald retreads
told me freedom
was on the other side of childhood.

-Benger

cold water glistens

we were raw souls
we didn't know it
sapling catalpas roam
subtropical summer sidewalks
desperate for a breath
inside the walls of swelter

there would be this electric
buzz rattling in the air
of our childhood bedrooms
our teeth would chatter simultaneous
then we would be in the streets
in our shorts, our underoos

the local fireman opened
the plugs, the water rushed
torrents along neighborhood curbs
all the kids were there
between parked car rapids
some feet in, some ass in
some attempt to swim
some erode into
the debris of the city

these little catalpas
inebriated in perfect equation
cold water glistens
meets summer afternoon
a still life in eternity

-baldinger

Legacy

We walked rails and
blew bubble gum into
our own faces.

We shot bb's at leaves and
smelled the slow burn of October.

We wiped out on our bikes
in gravel church parking lots and
practiced skateboard tricks
in friends' garages.

Up in the tree house, we
played Never Have I Ever
with the neighbor girl and
we talked dreams behind the gym.

We played flashlight tag in the field and
we made bonfires from algebra books.

We told scary stores over hot
chocolate and kerosene and
we felt bees in our arms.

Money was a box of Runts
and a glass of Dr. Pepper.

Love was for the now and
for the future.

Life was for us.

When it's all over,
no one can say
we didn't live.

-Benger

when noise was young

back when noise was young
pedal boards on dive bar stages
delay and distortion, the din of traffic
all those nothing doing saturdays
lost in feedback loops

practice space couches
overlook mexican markets
I was learning to carry
this city in my teeth then

the chain american diners
of our formative years
all night coffee and cigarettes
friendly cockroaches pull up a chair

gathered around a talkback mic
as the board bled red
needles never waver
acoustic guitars split speakers

twenty five years
how did we figure on
the places sounds left us
the communion found on stages
ears ringing at three am
still amped, drunk and bereft

last time we bumped into each other
is another memory condemned
you tell me the darkness
gets harder to swallow now
settles in longer, steals more
sometimes you just can't let it go

after your father's death
questions of gender reopen
these constructs never fit right
there's no one left to please now
except yourself

you re-introduce as calley
after years spent listless
living in skin that never fit right
working through a legal world
once you sign the papers
maybe find yourself in that drying ink
while another dead name drops away

-baldinger

Interlude:
Dreaming

The Old Girl

The old truck was going to give out,
I could feel it. The way the works
shimmied under the hood every time
I gave her some gas. The way the
whole damn thing would lurch
unnaturally whenever I downshifted.
This was not the time for a failure.
The snow was getting increasingly
fierce. A hail of massive, bluish-white
flakes, backlit by the halogens, waged
war on the old girl. No other drivers
were dumb enough to be on the road.
Conditions had been proclaimed
"undriveable" by the local newsman
hours ago. Still, I had places to be.
So I drove on. About once a minute,
the truck would do something that
would make me involuntarily hold
my breath. Each time, when I realized
what I was doing and corrected it, I
was gasping for what little oxygen
was left in the stale, overheated air
of the cab. Then the bald tires skidded
on the wet, treacherous road. The old
girl went right through the guardrail,
leaving the hood somewhere far behind.
Blue smoke shot from the truck's guts
in front of the windshield. I heard a
crunch, metal on life, and for the briefest

second, it all went black. Only for a
second, though. Then it was all light.
More than light; white. I looked out through
the now missing windshield, and the
storm had passed. The whole season
had passed. The grass was tall and
green in the ditch. Birds were shouting.
The sun was out, hot and wonderful.
I opened the old girl's driver's side
door, and it screamed a rusty protest.
I stepped onto the soft, perfect ground.
I walked to the rumpled front of the
truck. There was a coyote standing there,
inspecting what was left of the bumper.
Our eyes met, and I understood. The
coyote turned tail and began to slowly
amble away. After a second or two, I
followed. Someday, we'll get to
where we're going.

-Benger

the bay city blues

bay city, I was never so frail
overlooking that huron ocean
summer black flies swell
the debris of highways
down past grand funkin' flint
down river to detroit

I don't know when the end was
a steady erosion in the waves
this windblown son
taking that manifest birth right

I mean it had to be california
it's always california
bass unsettles the san andreas
frogs in the mouth of angel's camp sunsets

or in a dimly lit pizzeria
seventies red plastic
that hang on yreka nowhere
waiting on hummingbirds

I left it all out there somewhere
an iron range of miles mined
a boulder scatter still covered
waiting for the melt
that feeds those big rivers

waiting on the edge of yonder
until all that's left

is the paper lungs of ghosts
awestruck in loneliness
under a pink champlain sky

it's bay city again
another decade stretched til it broke
a downtown naked of visitors
on this marlow noir sunday
I may not he human

as the huron ocean stretches
all early spring breathless
another second to lose it all
if you seek a pleasant peninsula
look about you

-baldinger

Part II:

Searching for a Reason

Getting On

She has a whole lot of trouble
admitting that any of this
is of any reasonable consequence.

There's blood on the floor,
and she's not sure
how long it's been there,
or even who's it is,
though she's the only one
who's ever here, so...

Cars hiss by her window
just like in that old song,
but nothing about this is
sweet and bluesy,
though the crippling longing
has a place in all of this for sure.

She walked down the hall
a few days ago,
slid the rent check under a door,
sounds of soap opera
blaring from an antiquated tv
on the other side of the
cheap hollow wood,
and that trip seems like enough
to count as social interaction
for at least the rest of the week.

She's having trouble finding
a reason to look for a reason,
and all the while that maroon crust
not far from her bare mattress
calls to her,
some reminder that all of this
does have some consequence.

She tosses a soiled shirt over the stain,
and gets on with the business
of getting on.

-Benger

phil ochs' suicide note

they're shooting a hollywood
movie on my street corner
or some TV show that leans
into the grit and rust mantra
this town was known for

big cranes hold skylights
bright beams spill
into my kitchen
with its warped floor tiles
and leaky fridge
its daylight at 9pm
inches from the longest
night of the year

tortoise shell cat
in a paper bag
attacks a rolled ball
ten years ago
I had to hit pavement
as shots fired
we're close like yellow jackets

all those late-night fights
outside the six pack shop
would bring out red and blue
bubble gum machines
colored lights beat curtains

now yoga pants clad moms
run strollers up these hills
no loitering signs rust, ignored
no more woop woop whistles
no more shouts 5-0, 5-0

faceless billionaires graze avenue bones
I am at crest of the wave
reading death poems submissions
the zeitgeist of the moment
I settle into phil ochs' suicide note
blink rust out of my eyes

-baldinger

He Calls It A Life

He calls it a life.

Simple and pleasant,
quiet and humble.
He keeps to himself,
always has, and that
brings him little trouble.
Every now and then
the taxes rise,
or the new folks
down the block's terrier
will leave a pile
by the mailbox,
but that's not much,
not when one considers
how it could be,
how others,
less discreet others,
how their lives
always seem to turn out
flames and blood and fireworks.

He calls it a life.

Thought about getting a cat once,
but that was only
a passing fancy.
Who would want
all that cleanup,
all that commitment.

He's got his perennials out front,
his potted lotus in the entryway
for a taste of the exotic.
Once in a while,
he'll get some takeout
(outrageous prices, but he's heard
one must splurge a little)
every few months.

He calls it a life.

Detached garage
with everything always in its place,
paving stones around the perimeter,
just the same.
Leaves are never in his gutters,
the gas in the red can
never goes flat,
oil never sits long enough to stain.
He let a hairline cracked
basement window go once
for nearly a week,
and that private shame
still haunts him something awful.

He calls it a life.

Simple meals in the kitchen,
same plate always
immediately washed.
Thermostat at 78 in the summer,
65 in the winter, nearly always

just one shade left of comfortable.
Hotel art on walls,
evenly spaced,
balsa and tack frames.
The bed is always quiet, neat,
hospital corners, and
just as antiseptic.

He calls it a life,
but she didn't,
and every night before
the dark takes him down,
he wonders.

-Benger

barely living patriots

I can't place the name
of my friend's dog who died
embarrassed stoned splutters
stuck on loki
a dog I briefly shared
with an old girlfriend
back in another century

now stuck in my throat
that bitter ash of a bleak year
spent working nights at wal mart
for minimum plus shift differential
holed up in a trailer in beaver county
with a girl named kara
her menagerie of stray animals
the dead lights of deepening depression
circled with friends barely hanging on

flashes of seasons
seen through dawn rides home
blurred exhaustion of bare trees
there is no summer
only the fourth of july
azure sky deepens
before fireworks glitter and pop
she's giving me a hand job
on the hill behind the elementary
school in a town called
zelienople

let's welcome this next new year
barely living patriots
choke on acrid small town air
thick humid gunpowder smoke
happy birthday america
exactly how am I free?

-baldinger

Edge

She sleeps on the
edge of the mattress.
Never intends to,
that's just where she always is
when she wakes up.
Doesn't matter much;
not like that mattress is on
anything higher than the ground.

It's been this way for too long;
always on the edge of something,
but never quite there.
Always stagnating,
never any kind of
cleansing resurgence.

The cigarettes are stale,
the subway piss is stale,
the exhaust always
looming in the air is stale,
the tips at the club are stale,
the men's half-assed,
entitled advances are stale,
the lonely bourbon afterward is stale,
the edge of the mattress is stale.

Everything about life is.

So much so,
she begins to wonder if maybe
it's not life,
but her.

She thinks she can remember a time
when things made sense,
and when they didn't,
it didn't matter,
because it really didn't.

Now nothing adds up,
and everything matters,
and nothing is right,
and she's not sure she understands
the words "clean" and "fresh"
in anything other than
the most academic sense.
The word "hope" is
worse than a lost cause,
it's a Goddamned lie.

She woke up on the edge of the mattress,
but at least there's
nowhere else to fall.

-Benger

the last vestige of tiki

carla limes then salts corona bottlenecks
professional bartender gauntlet
she's been at this for centuries
I count the hayseeds
think about nicotine
time stamped into the grass skirts
that may be the last vestige of tiki
left in this motel lounge

she left this town for philly
as soon as she grew wings
bounced around holiday inns
with private dancer as soundtrack
acquired all the merit badges
service time affords
she's been rubies and diamonds
she's been gold club

but the city will wear on a heart
the service industry takes what it will
so she left it and a no good man
to come back home
bought in on unincorporated land
dark skies and nowhere
far enough from the ghost of her memories

she keeps company
with a man from another small town
somewhere dusty like oklahoma

where they only drink
tomato juice and budweiser

tonight it's everyone's birthday
off kilter and out of key
sounding like an am radio
commercial for the rural king

I cash out after I hit my limit
tip amounts to the check
carla and I wish each other luck
I'll sleep deeply tonight
wrapped in red and wildflower smoke

-baldinger

11:59

he spends his nights
and no small part of his days
worrying, thinking, pining
on the nature of mortality,
specifically his own.

he prays for some kind of
unattainable dispensation;
some kind of reprieve
from inevitable decay.

because he's not done,
it's not done,
and at the end of each day,
he's increasingly aware
that it never will be.

he smells his end
getting closer with
each exhalation,
and he knows there's
nothing to be done.

forestall it, sure,
negate it, never.

and for that,
his nights are sweaty,
repugnant reminders

of a flailing, falling day.

he swears he will
live before he dies.

but the clock refuses
to tick any slower.

-Benger

god is back in town

power of love
follows *ghostbusters*
joe namath sells
medicare suppliments
now *voices carry*
for the third time
in less than a week
it might be 1985
except I'm in youngstown
sipping a negroni
not nine years old
with no concrete
understanding of time

god is back in town
other than thunderstorms
there's no evidence of a deity
only empty streets
bars where the keep
named their cats
after the former president
and his first lady

I want to give my beer back
walk through the dark
of the pool room
into lightning strikes
heat evaporates
in fat drops of rain

I leap the river
along the curb
hope to spot a penguin
days past what doesn't feel
like my 45th birthday
still no concrete
understanding of time

-baldinger

Dust

She pretends to remember a time
when all of this monotony
didn't seem so preordained.
Tries to fool herself into believing
that there was once a moment
when although nothing was right,
there was a wistful hope of
regaining her perpetually shaky equilibrium.

There is a thick layer of dust
on top of the tv,
and exponentially more
on the windowsill.
Nothing is clean anymore,
everything so far gone,
any kind of restoration
feels like the sickest of jokes.

Hope feels a like a cruel barb;
something to bleed her out
as the entire world
rolls their eyes and laughs.
Because to them, she's not real.

To herself,
she wonders if she ever was.

-Benger

the half-life of lead

black walls fold into the infinity
of a jefferson city sunset
books lit by a candle
streetlights dot an empty bluff
this block of parked cars and dive bars
it was the perfect time to sneak
in the community center
steal a shower, a sliver of soap
knowing dali and lolita
waltz across the embouchure
of ceres' capital dome

I've been waiting with the wind
for those three hours a week
let those black walls crowd
full typeset wanders
moldering pages return to atoms
the half-life of lead

an old hippie materializes
shrubs in his beard
remembers his arrival on the dog star
his 1975 stories between meters
end in a puff of smoke

some century all those hours
will add up to a year
old ladies in attics dig out gold
the forgotten prose

the poetry expansion packs
wisdom set on the pages
met with laughter between
swigs of gas station sweet tea

there are worlds of wonder
we'll never know anything about
if only there was capital left in wisdom
if only we had something left
worth saying about time
something more than
an ink shadow disappeared

-baldinger

Corners

She finds corners to be the best.
No one bothers,
no one attacks,
no one talks,
offers help,
gives advice,
promises how good the world is
outside of the corner.

She finds corners to be the best.
Dark,
lonely,
claustrophobic
as they are,
they are hers,
and no one sees,
so no will
take them from her.

-Benger

a narrative of bloodshot

hungover in khakis
or still drunk and past thirty
fifteen minutes late for every shift
in a nowhere called west mifflin
this desert island hell
a retail oasis

drug store third key
has shards left
a life in pieces
at ten dollars an hour
enough take home
to split rent three ways
in a four bedroom hovel
fast food sustenance
a case of beer every few days
always some cheap
macrobrew pisswater
that with enough motivation
obliterates the memory
of another 6am shift
shuffling blue plastic tubs
down a conveyor belt
as breath plumes freeze
of another 3pm shift
shouted down by food stamps
and dragon soccer moms
of another overnight
setting shelves with
that hot new product line

everyday bleeds into
a narrative of bloodshot
a monolith of the same halogen
the same calming grey tones
the same forgotten one hits
that hum along through sleep

keep on drinking
keep it numb
watch the zombies
shuffle for more drugs
to keep them undead
through their myriad disasters

light another cigarette
sniff at the laundry
hope it's clean enough
to last another shift
a couple more ibuprofen
to settle the grinding metal
bile rising and it's time
another forty hours lost
another shift broken
another forty hours lost
another shift broke

-baldinger

tear

he can't let go of it
that old rag
crusted with blood
lingering in the bedroom
of his single wide

that blue and white trailer
which is every day
sinking further into the mud

and sure it's his blood
but she put it there
or at least started the flow
that necessitated the
ripped scrap of linen

there might've been
plenty of consuming fire
in their brief time
but there were also
fireworks

and though the rag came from
destruction
it conjures memories
of quiet nights
of boxed wine
and whispered promises

he thinks of the rag
touches the scar
above his lip
and dreams of a future
rooted in their past

-Benger

hymn to a pittsburgh toilet

I used to look willie nelson
in the eye every time
I took a shit

willie taped to a stall door
deep lines in his face
years of bad shows, pot busts
life's tragedies writ large

when I was hungover, I'd whistle
blue eyes crying in the rain

that toilet was what we call
a pittsburgh toilet
an ode to mill hunk roots
a toilet open and exposed
in a dank low ceiling basement
filled with 40 years
of forgotten record store debris

this toilet was no longer authentic
a crude plywood enclosure
offered tenuous privacy

above the commode
a picture of fish
derek william dick not abe vigoda
singer of a faintly remembered
english prog band

one sheet of fish
candid answers on
streaking after bad decisions
hecklers pulling knives
I'll spare you the rest

that storefront sells kratom now
after selling shoes, then records
for the better part of a century

fred rose or willie, they were right
only memories remain

                    -baldinger

vocal

she finds peace
in the stream
out in the woods
on the other side of the tracks
outside of the park

that same stream
where many of the denizens
find a truth
outside of the bottle
or the pipe
or the fists

brown water trickling
she sinks to her knees
and almost prays
to the water
to herself
maybe even to a god

more than anything
she prays to
the force in herself
the willingness
the need to
keep on

eyes closed
knees in leaves and mud

she chants
don't leave me
please don't leave me

it goes on so long
she never notices
when she begins to
say it out loud

-Benger

only black and white dreams

my cat, new to birding
stalks three television crows
they rummage at winter
she's dressed for murder

previously she stood
atop flat screen
confused
there was no way
to attack the data
found in a bird of paradise

I tell her I have a hard time with reality too
camera cuts to robert frank
who talks americans
those wide-open spaces
only black and white dreams fill

a sound runs in my head
shrill, pitched, fierce
same sound unzipped me
on a cold north dakota morning

two mustangs
battle for supremacy
buck and rear
the futility of territory
which gladiator won is irrelevant

it's 6:30 in the badlands
I might suggest they
gallop to town
buy each other a round
talk out their anger
then cool it in a hotwalker

robert frank says
it was all wide open once
he says it without malice
as if an ill wind never once
blew through buffalo grass

-baldinger

Part III:

What We Have

incremental

follow the road
into the negative spaces
where light turns in itself
refracting into black
as the miasma of
our sluggish existence
peters its way to a slow crawl

dew drops on rusted rails
the shed bark of the fir tree
an old horseshoe and cowbell
buried in a century of forgotten moments

there is a wall that
separates all of this
claims it for its own
a universe under the paper

as we peer the bugs crawl
and all the cogs
turn brilliantly clockwork

but one can't polish a rock
without some important tumbling

the quartz of us
finds itself more useless

when in meaningless pieces
but anything can pave a road

even the ones that lead out

-Benger

a howard johnson's prayer

nothing has a right being this beautiful
in the mighty exhale
of crossing the heartland again
the chill that saturates
post labor day
the sun already a victim
but there are no stars
in this fenced pool
parking lot watering hole
with logos looming
and billboards crowing
and traffic blowing past
headlights through honeycomb
and the interstate close enough
to hear it whinny at the horizon

another outlaw moment
flat earth and flood plain
250 miles and 25 mg
waiting on the corn stalks
to colonize these temples

cold blue water steals
as it reinforces this essence
I float on dreams that stretch
middle mississippi to machu picchu
I float a black and white dream
memories of dark sky meditations

-baldinger

disposable

everything is a commercial
vying for the money
that so few have

bright shiny comeons
for all the unnecessary
filling us with dissatisfaction

as an empire crumbles
as the animals die
as each sunrise

seems more unlikely
than the last
we weep

and click subscribe
and dream
of the disposable

-Benger

the aforementioned skyline

neither drugs or sunglasses best
parking lot halogen in sharonville
men sleep in their cars
groggy groundhog heads
pop up as people pass

this cheap motel surrounded
the other motel rustles
behind the tree line
the waffle house gives way
to skyline chili, to fast food
to big box chains
without a compass
there are no bearings
just endless small towns
swallowed by a shadow city

waffle house takes out the trash
street cats shake
out of a lilac bush
skinny and skittery
about to take over the night

there is a pound of cheddar in the plastic
to go bag of the aforementioned skyline
too lazy to head south
toward the clang
of the underground railroad

I eat in my room
with cigarettes and black mold
as a representative of wealth
I lay out a shredded trail
a dairy bar feast
a transient gift
a yellow orange supply
to sustain a brood of hungry meows

consider it an offering
a small good thing
to bring the rain

-baldinger

Grayson, MO

The houses squat together,
singular testaments to
giving up.

A line in the dirt,
in and out and
not much more.

Dealership high on the hill,
more trucks than
residents in the town,
post office maximum occupancy:
five in a pinch.

It's a good place to go
if money's not a concern,
and you never want to be found.

-Benger

sixty cycle hum

either it's the longest january
or the shortest year in history
here in the copper of winter
at the end of the world again

cracking open a map
the big game turns to newsprint
tweakers sweep across
a cracker barrel lot
itchy rain soaked neon
at midnight orion tunes in motown

gas station crème brûlée
my life as a machine at rest
listening to a 1956 thunderstorm
drench through to 57, maybe
liner note rivers idle in mascara

if I'm gone too long
or I get lost somewhere deep
say in 70s burgundy
or appalachian folktale
please pull me back
before my mustache hits the floor

at the end of my legs
I retreat to nostrums and magic
kill the engine in the walnut flats
water over shoals
maintains a sixty cycle hum

as anesthetic wears on
we look like our mothers at dawn
lap full of guitar
metronome clicking 'til
a freight train derails
has anyone else noticed
the drop ceiling they installed in the sky?

-baldinger

Spiral

Everything changes hands
but little is ever heard;

everything mixing as it does
with the emotional wind and rain,

and humanity pilots itself one way,
while the earth heads somewhere else,

drifting ever further from one another,
searching, searching, but never finding,

sun goes dimmer as the
noise gets louder,

and no communication
save screams

are heard,
but no one really ever hears even them

for what they truly are:
the final cries from a long-suffering

entity of life,
and the fires keep burning,

and the fiddles screech,
and what doesn't incinerate

drowns and sinks to the bottom,
sand up nostrils,

the cleanest thing in decades.

-Benger

across greyscale scrub

I felt the ocean rolling
in blood for the last month
the timeliness of tradition
grows into a throb
until highways dismantle
rattle of traffic
chunks of pavement
disappear into salt air
into the crash of waves
into the approximate
or infinite

with the moonrise
it will all look different
boardwalk lights
fade to constellation

somehow eight years run
across the horizon
as one moment
heat lightning brain
meets cold air deepening

I still have my prayers
maybe more than ever
left in the sand
pulled back by the tide

I have a year to dissolve
trusting time is water soluble

horseshoe crab shells moored
sand prints across motel carpet
across greyscale scrub
another sunset in the sideview
another sunrise witnessed
another year piles on graceless
listening to waves break
across the highways
through the heartland
along the shore

-baldinger

Inventory

What we have is a handful of nothing.

What we have is all those last chances.

What we have is balled up into a tight fist of regret.

What we have is nothing, nothing.

What we have binds us to what we don't.

What we have are promises itching to be broken.

What we have are bones and dust.

What we have pretends comfort only to strike.

What we have once passed for virtue.

What we have played piano on the back steps.

What we have saw all and lied about it.

What we have stirs guts for the fun of it.

What we have buries us in longing.

What we have peeks from under the bed.

What we have is fractured memories.

What we have is us.

What we have is enough.

                    -Benger

a time capsule of dust

nefertiti smiles
miles davis stares stage left
through matte black wood bins
in a spartan store
in a depressed town
church spires through windows
and an always vacant stage

this is a time capsule of dust
forgotten side street
where stock is stale and still
where lps are albatross
new formats bring abandon

I come weekly, skipping class
slow graze imagine
sounds from covers
liner notes conjuring
slowly eating inventory
slowly building vocabulary

six bucks is a princely sum
by mid-nineties standards
but a small price for fraternity
and maybe I didn't know
that's what I was buying

at the counter, a big man
basso buddha with diabetes
gruff voiced wrestler expounds

from the stacks of a library mind
he always has some insignificant minutiea
that leads to a dead afternoon
conversation, sound and vision
I'm picking his brain
expanding beyond my ears
as I said it's building vocabulary

years later I would run into him
another record store dying
our roles reversed
I would remind him
of those afternoons lost
how they led me here
to my own library mind
as I said it's about fraternity

there is a clumsy grace
in the moments where
we find ourselves
chrysalis and seed pods
blowing in breezes around
creeks named connoquenessing
traffic flowing past
formative forgotten spaces

sometimes there no words
for our shepherds, those people
who cling at the outskirts
with the tenacity of ghosts

-baldinger

James Benger has written a bunch of stuff. Some of it has even been published in print and on the interwebs. So far there are two ebooks, three chapbooks, six splits, and two full-lengths. He is the resident slacker on the Board of Directors of the Writers Place, and is the most truant member of the Riverfront Readings Committee. He is also the admin of an online poetry workshop called 365 Poems in 365 Days, which has produced four anthologies and counting. He lives in Kansas City with his wife and children.

Jason Baldinger is a poet and photographer from Pittsburgh, PA. He is the co-editor of *Trailer Park Quarterly* and co-runs The Odd-Month Reading Series. He's penned twenty books of poetry the newest of which include: *A History of Backroads Misplaced: Selected Poems 2010-2020* (Kung Fu Treachery), *American Aorta* (OAC Books) and a forthcoming collection *Waiting on Hummingbirds* with Kansas poet James Benger (Their fourth together) His first book of photography, *Lazarus* (OAC Books), was released last year and the ekphrastic collaboration *Hope is a Prison* with poet Rebecca Schumejda (Kung Fu Treachery) just hit bookstores. More ekphrastic collaborations are in the works featuring his photography in 2025. His poems and photos have appeared across a wide variety of online sites and print journals. You can hear him read from various books on Bandcamp and on lps by The Gotobeds and Theremonster.

This project was made possible, in part, by generous support from the Osage Arts Community.

Osage Arts Community provides temporary time, space and support for the creation of new artistic works in a retreat format, serving creative people of all kinds — visual artists, composers, poets, fiction and nonfiction writers. Located on a 152-acre farm in an isolated rural mountainside setting in Central Missouri and bordered by ¾ of a mile of the Gasconade River, OAC provides residencies to those working alone, as well as welcoming collaborative teams, offering living space and workspace in a country environment to emerging and mid-career artists. For more information, visit us at www.osageac.org

Osage Arts Community